BRITAIN IN WORLD WAR II

Rationing

Alison Cooper

Based on an original text by
Fiona Reynoldson

HODDER
Wayland

an imprint of Hodder Children's Books

BRITAIN IN WORLD WAR II
Titles in this series
THE BLITZ
EVACUATION
RATIONING
WOMEN'S WAR

Original design: Nick Cannan
Differentiated design: Raynor Design
This title designed by: Joy Mutter
Text consultant: Norah Granger

Based on an original text *The Home Front – Rationing*, by Fiona Reynoldson, published in 1990 by Wayland Publishers Ltd

This edition published in 2003 by Hodder Wayland, an imprint of Hodder Children's Books

British Library Cataloguing in Publication Data
Cooper, Alison, 1967 - Rationing. - Differentiated ed. - (Britain in World War II)1. World War, 1939-1945 - Food supply - Great Britain - Juvenile literature 2. Rationing - Great Britain - History - 20th century - Juvenile literature 3. World War, 1939-1945 - Social aspects - Great Britain - Juvenile literature 4. Great Britain - Social conditions - 20th century - Juvenile literature I. Title II. Reynoldson, Fiona 941'.084

ISBN 0 7502 4305 8

Printed and bound by G. Canale & C. S.p.A. - Borgaro T.se - Turin

Hodder Children's Books
a division of Hodder Headline Limited
338 Euston Road, London NW1 3BH

 See page 31 for ways in which you can use this book to encourage literacy skills.

Acknowledgements
The publishers would like to thank the following for permission to reproduce their pictures: ET Archive 8, 26; Mary Evans Picture Library 6 (right); Hulton Picture Library 4 (below), 7, 9 (above), 11, 12, 21 (right), 22 (right), 25 (left), 27 (above), 28 (both); Imperial War Museum 4 (above), 10, 17 (right), 21 (left); Peter Newark 6 (left), 15 (above), 17 (left), 18 (above), 24, 25 (right); Popperfoto 19; Punch 14, 22 (left); Topham Picture Library 9 (below), 13, 15 (below), 16, 18 (below), 20, 23, 29; Weimar Archive 27 (below). The artwork is by John Yates. Cover image: used with the permission of the Trustees of the Imperial War Museum, London, D25035.

Contents

Preparing for War

We risk our lives to bring you food. It's up to you not to waste it.

'A Message from our Seamen'

▲ This poster from the First World War warns people not to waste food.

In the late 1930s people realized that soon there would be a war in Europe. Britain prepared for a long, hard fight against Germany. Factories began to produce new aeroplanes, ships and guns.

The government knew that German aircraft would drop bombs on cities. So they made plans to send city children away to safer places. They also knew that German submarines would sink ships bringing food to Britain. To make sure that everyone would still get enough to eat, they set up a system called rationing.

▶ This woman is checking piles of ration books. Everyone had to have a ration book during the Second World War.

Adult's Weekly Ration in May, 1941.

3 pints milk

55 g tea

one shilling's worth meat

225 g jam

170 g butter

55 g cooking fat

225 g sugar

115 g bacon

30 g cheese

▲ This picture shows the weekly ration for an adult in May 1941. The amount of rations was set for four weeks at a time.

Rationing was a way of giving everyone a fair share of certain basic foods, such as meat and cheese. The government brought in rules that said how much basic food each person could buy each week. Some foods, such as bread, were not rationed.

Rationing was not a new idea. It had been used at the end of the First World War (1914-1918).

Organizing Rationing

Rationing was organized by the Ministry of Food, which was a government department. One man who worked for the ministry explained: 'It was run by people who knew about buying, selling and storing goods such as bacon, ham, butter, tea and so on'. The ministry organized the storage and distribution of food around the country, and was divided into different sections. Each section bought large amounts of a particular type of food. For example, the Bacon and Ham Division bought meat supplies.

▼ This cartoon from 1942 shows two burglars at work. They are more interested in stealing ration coupons than money.

▼ This is the front cover of a ration book.

"Nothing but money, money, money! Where the blazes do they keep their coupons?"

ON HIS MAJESTY'S SERVICE

OFFICIAL PAID

Your Ration Book

Issued to safeguard your food supply

HOLDER'S NAME AND REGISTERED ADDRESS

COMPARE WITH YOUR IDENTITY CARD AND REPORT ANY DIFFERENCE TO YOUR FOOD OFFICE — DO NOT ALTER

Surname ......TAPPENDEN......

Other Names ...J. Margaret...

Address ...58. Beansfield Rd...

...SE 3....

NAT. REG. NO. ...AHAV 369 2...

Date of Issue ...7 JUL 1941...   Serial Number of Book

If found, please return to

GREENWICH PS 728578

FOOD OFFICE.   R.B.1 [General] 4

Ration books

Every household had to fill in a form saying how many people lived in their house. They sent it to their local food office. There was usually a food office in every town. The staff at the food office sent a ration book to each person.

When people went to buy food, they had to show the shopkeeper their ration book. The shopkeeper sold them the amount of food they were allowed to have. Then the shopkeeper cut out the coupon to show that the ration had been used.

Healthy Eating

Before the war a lot of people did not eat very healthy foods. Often, poor families could not afford good food. The Ministry of Food wanted to improve people's diets. Its Scientific Division worked out what kind of nutrients people needed for good health. Children and pregnant women were given extra milk, cod-liver oil and orange juice to improve their health.

▼ Doctor Carrot and Potato Pete were cartoon characters who encouraged people to grow and eat more vegetables.

◀ Many people grew vegetables and kept some hens, so that they did not have to rely only on their rations.

The basal diet

If German submarines sank a lot of cargo ships, there was a danger that there might not be enough food, even though it was rationed. The Scientific Division worked out the smallest amount of food that people needed to survive. It was called the basal diet and it was made up of bread, potatoes, oatmeal, vegetables and milk. The scientists even suggested that people could eat unusual foods such as dandelion fritters or nettle toast.

Winston Churchill, the British Prime Minister, thought the basal diet sounded dreadful! He said a diet like that would make people so miserable that Britain would lose the war.

▼ Rationing brought a better standard of food for people, and many babies born during the war were healthier than babies born before the war.

'Milk of course, but don't forget Cod Liver Oil & Orange Juice'

WELFARE FOODS SERVICE

The Battle of the Atlantic

Vital supplies were brought to Britain from the USA, Canada and Britain's colonies in the Caribbean. Some ships that crossed the Atlantic carried food. Others carried machinery, weapons and fuel. Without fuel Britain would not be able to use its warships and aircraft.

The Germans knew how important it was to stop supplies reaching Britain. In 1941 the German Admiral Dönitz said, 'With enough U-boats [submarines] we can and will finish off the British Isles.'

Convoys

Ships carrying supplies made the dangerous journey across the Atlantic in convoys. This means that they sailed in large groups, with warships to protect them. But U-boat captains became very good at hunting down convoys. Several U-boats would attack a convoy at the same time. The warships could not protect all the supply ships at once. At the worst time, during 1942, one in every four supply ships was sunk.

▼ This poster reminds people that sailors risked their lives to bring them supplies. It was vital not to waste anything.

▼ A convoy of twenty-four ships in the North Sea.

Attacks on the Docks

When ships did reach Britain safely the precious supplies were unloaded at the docks and stored. London was a very big port, used by many ships. Docks lined the banks of the River Thames.

At the docks there were huge warehouses where different goods were stored, such as meat, flour, sugar and wood.

▶ A ship being unloaded in the London docks.

The Blitz

The Germans knew how important these warehouses were. Night after night during the Blitz they bombed the London docks. Blazing warehouses lit up the sky.

To protect the supplies, some ships were sent to other, safer ports, instead of London. Goods were unloaded and sent across the country by train. Some ships still had to be unloaded in the London docks. The goods were moved quickly to warehouses in the countryside so that they would not be destroyed by bombs. At one time, flour was put into big barges and towed up the River Thames, away from the docks area.

▲ The London docks on fire after a night of bombing on 7 September 1940.

Shopping and Cooking

The idea of rationing was that everyone would get a fair share of basic foods, such as milk, meat and sugar. Many foods were not rationed, but they were hardly ever on sale in the shops. One woman explained: 'Sometimes you could get fish but it was always in short supply – first come, first served. You could wait half an hour in the queue and still not get any.'

It was nearly always women who did the shopping and cooking. Planning the best way to use the rations took a lot of time.

▶ There were not enough ingredients to make big wedding cakes so people had to make do with pretend ones made of cardboard.

...Shoot straight, Lady

◄ This poster reminded people that housewives had an important job to do in helping Britain to win the war. They had to use the rations carefully and keep everyone well fed.

People had to get used to cooking with different ingredients, too. Dried fruit for cakes was in very short supply. One woman said: 'We used to go and collect elderberries in autumn. When we dried them we could use them instead of currants for a cake.'

Another wartime ingredient was dried egg. Eggs sent to Britain by ship from the USA had to be dried so that they did not go bad on the journey.

◄ People could buy a cheap meal in a British Restaurant without using coupons. This helped to make the rations at home last longer.

Digging for Victory

The Ministry of Food wanted people to grow as much food as possible. Britain would then not need to rely so much on supplies brought by ship. Posters were put up telling people to 'Dig for Victory'.

By 1943 there were one and a half million allotments in Britain. People also grew vegetables in gardens, at the side of railways, in window boxes and on the roofs of their 'Anderson shelters' (air-raid shelters). One man described how they kept 'chickens at the end of the garden and rabbits in a hutch. The rabbits were to eat and we used the fur for gloves.'

► These people could get fresh eggs from their own chickens.

▲ A 'Dig for Victory' poster.

▲ Vegetables were even grown in famous parks such as Hyde Park in London.

The Ministry of Food told people how to cook with their home-grown vegetables. Every morning a radio programme called *Kitchen Front* gave out recipe ideas. Lord Woolton, the head of the Ministry of Food, invented 'Lord Woolton's Pie'. It was filled with vegetables and topped with potatoes.

Farming Round the Clock

▲ A poster asking women to join the Land Army and go to work on farms.

▼ These women are planting potatoes.

Growing vegetables and keeping chickens in the garden was one way of producing more food but it was not enough. Farmers had to produce a lot more food too. Ten million acres of grassland were ploughed up to grow wheat and other crops. New machines were introduced, and farmers even fitted lights to their ploughs, so that they could plough at night as well as in the daytime.

In 1939, Britain produced only 40 per cent of the food it needed. The rest had to be brought by ship from other countries. By 1945 Britain was able to produce 60 per cent of the food it needed.

One big problem for the government was the shortage of workers. Many farm workers had left their jobs at the start of the war to join the army, navy or air force. During the First World War women had done a lot of work on farms, so in 1939 the government set up the Women's Land Army again. One woman described how she spent all day lifting potatoes: 'At first my back ached like mad but I got used to it and loved the outdoor life.'

▲ Two women from the Land Army using a reaping machine.

Make Do and Mend

By June 1941 Britain had been at war for almost two years. Now even clothes, material and shoes had to be rationed. To buy clothes people had to spend coupons as well as money. For instance, a man's shirt was 5 coupons, a jacket 13 coupons and a tie one coupon. Each person had 66 clothing coupons to last them a year. Later in the war the number was reduced to 48. People had to use their coupons to buy goods such as sheets and towels, as well as clothes.

► People could not buy many new clothes during the war but they had to have a hat if they wanted to look smart.

▲ This government poster encourages housewives to mend clothes instead of buying new ones.

▲ Even wartime furniture was plain and simple, to avoid using too much wood.

People had to mend their old clothes if they could. The government made films showing how to cut up a man's old coat to make a child's coat. They even suggested saving flour sacks to make a girl's dress.

New clothes had to be made from as little material as possible. Women's skirts and dresses were short and plain so that they did not use too much material. Shirts could not have more than four buttons. One woman said the wartime clothes were 'simple, plain and neat and we got terribly tired of them'.

The Black Market

Most people thought rationing was a good idea and they did not try to get more than their fair share. But some people were prepared to steal goods and sell them secretly. Other people were willing to pay a high price for the stolen goods. This secret buying and selling was called the black market.

▼ In this cartoon Mr Black the market gardener is upset because the sign writer has made it look as if he is involved in the black market.

▼ American soldiers were popular in Britain because they often had supplies that British people could not get. These Americans are handing out toys at Christmas.

"Hi—what about a comma or something after my name?"

Some people stole just a few small items. One train driver explained how they sometimes stole a box of fish to make themselves a good supper: 'We'd have a couple of haddock, or four kippers, on a shovel cooked up in the engine.'

Stealing from warehouses, docks and factories was more serious. About a million pounds worth of goods were stolen during 1941.

The black market was a problem in Britain. But it was never as big as the black market in other parts of Europe, where life was much harder.

▲ These women are queuing to buy food. Rationing made life difficult but most people just put up with it.

More Shortages

As the war went on, many goods became harder and harder to find. Paper was in short supply and envelopes had to be used over and over again. There were shortages of glass too. Some people owned their own cars, but after 1942 they could not get petrol to run them. All the petrol was needed for vehicles that were being used for war work.

People even had to ration the amount of time they spent listening to their radios. In the 1940s radios had valves that wore out and had to be replaced. It was very hard to get new valves. People had to make sure they turned their radios off if they were not really listening.

▼ This is an advertisement for Spam. Tinned meat like this was easy to transport and store.

Points rationing

In November 1941 the government introduced a new system of points rationing. Certain foods were worth a set number of points. Everyone was allowed to use sixteen points a month, as well as their normal ration coupons. They could spend their points on any kind of food they liked.

Biscuits, cereals, dried eggs and tinned fish and meat were all available on points rationing. Some people liked to save their points to buy luxuries. One man remembered how his mother saved up their points to buy a tin of fruit at Christmas.

CARELESS LISTENING?

CARELESS LISTENING COSTS VALVES

Nobody knows who turned the radio *on* — nobody's *listening* . . . so turn it OFF!

The radio gives grand entertainment, but if you're not actually *listening* . . . *switch off!* The Government ask everybody to save electricity, so don't keep your radio going unnecessarily.

Remember, too, that valves are difficult to replace when they ultimately wear out. So give the ones you've got every possible chance.

There are many thousands of fortunate owners of Mullard Sets and Valves who have proved the lasting value of their choice; for years they have enjoyed trouble-free, true-tone listening. That is why, when Victory is won and supplies are again available, they will still choose . . . MULLARD.

MULLARD
RADIO VALVES AND SETS

▲ This advertisement from a radio company reminds people to turn their radios off if they are not really listening.

◄ Anything that could be used again or recycled was collected. These boys have been collecting waste paper, bottles and tins.

Rationing in Germany

Rationing began in Germany in 1939. The weekly ration per person was one pound (454 g) of meat, five pounds (2.2 kg) of bread, 12 ounces (340 g) of fats, 12 ounces of sugar and one pound of ersatz coffee. Ersatz coffee was made from roasted barley seeds and acorns.

At that early stage of the war people could eat quite well. There was plenty of bread, for example. Every time the Germans conquered another country, trainloads of supplies were sent back to Germany.

► This is a ration card and an identity card. They belonged to a French person. The Germans introduced rationing when they conquered France.

▲ This picture shows someone digging out a supply of potatoes from the ruins of a house that has been bombed.

▼ An advertisement for Volkswagen cars from before the war. The German people were not able to afford such luxuries for many years after the war.

5 Mark die Woche musst Du sparen
willst Du im eignen Wagen fahren!

Petrol rationing was very strict, right from the beginning of the war. Clothes were rationed too. Shoes were in very short supply. People were only allowed to have two pairs. They had to show that one pair was worn out before they could buy any new ones. After 1942 the war started to go badly for Germany. Life became harder for the German people. Rations got smaller and smaller.

World Shortages

Britain and Germany were not the only countries where there were food shortages during the war. Food was scarce everywhere in Europe. In some countries, especially Poland, Greece and Yugoslavia, people really struggled to find enough to eat.

▼ It was much harder for people living in bombed cities, like Cologne in Germany, to get food than for people in the countryside.

▼ Food officers in Germany after the war, questioning a farmer's wife. Many farmers preferred to exchange their food for goods such as coffee or shoes, instead of selling it.

◄ The USA sent large amounts of food, like these supplies of sugar, to European countries after the war. This help was called Marshall Aid.

The fighting made it hard to produce enough food. In some areas farmland was turned into battlefields. Railway lines and roads were bombed, so food could not be moved to places where it was needed. Supply ships were sunk. A German rhyme from the time said:
'The rain will wash us all away,
Men as thin and pale as ghosts,
Rations smaller every day.'

The war in the Far East affected food supplies there, too. There was famine in some parts of India and China in 1943. Even when the war ended, things did not get better straight away. The USA sent food supplies but it was years before Europe, the Soviet Union and the Far East recovered.

Glossary

allotment A piece of land where people grow vegetables and fruit.

Anderson shelter An air-raid shelter that people built in their gardens. A big hole was dug in the ground and covered by a curved roof made from corrugated steel. Earth was then piled on top.

Blitz The bombing of British towns and cities by German aircraft in 1940-41.

colonies Countries that are ruled by another country.

coupon A small piece of paper, like a ticket.

famine A severe shortage of food.

nutrients Things that the body needs to get from food to stay healthy, such as proteins, fats and vitamins.

ration book A book full of coupons that people needed to show in order to buy certain foods.

reaping machine A machine used for cutting wheat or other cereal crops.

submarine A ship designed to travel underwater.

Projects

1. Look back to the illustration of wartime rations from May 1941. Weigh out the rations (ask permission first) to see how much of these basic foods an adult was allowed each week.

2. Today we buy a lot of cakes and biscuits from shops but in the 1940s most people baked their own. Look in a modern recipe book and see how much sugar and butter or margarine you need to make a sponge cake, or some buns. If you only had the wartime ration of sugar and butter, would you be able to make a cake? Could you make more than one?

3. Ask your older relatives or family friends if they can remember any wartime foods that they especially liked or disliked. Do they remember dried eggs, for example? Did any of them ever try Lord Woolton's pie?

Books to Read

The History Detective Investigates Rationing by Martyn Parsons (Hodder Wayland, 2000)
Make Do and Mend by Jack Wood (Watts, 2002)
Rationing by Stewart Ross (Evans, 2002)
Wartime Cookbook by Anne and Brian Moses (Hodder Wayland, 1998)

Places to Visit

Eden Camp, Malton, North Yorkshire YO17 6RT. Tel: 01653 697777.
This museum is based in an old army camp. It tells you about everyday life in the Second World War.

Imperial War Museum, Lambeth Road, London SE1 6HZ. Tel: 0207 416 5320.
This museum covers all aspects of life in the Second World War.

Winston Churchill's Britain at War Experience, 64-66 Tooley St, London Bridge, London SE1 2TF. Tel: 0207 403 3171.
In this museum you can see wartime goods on sale in a London street and find out more about rationing.

Use this book for teaching literacy

This book can help you in the literacy hour in the following ways:

- ✓ Children can use the contents page, page numbers, headings, captions and index to locate a particular piece of information.
- ✓ Posters, advertisements and newspaper headlines are good examples of the different styles of writing needed for Year 4 literacy teaching.
- ✓ Children can use the glossary to reinforce their alphabetic knowledge and extend their vocabulary.
- ✓ They can compare this book with fictional stories about World War II and rationing, to show how similar information can be presented in different ways.

Index

Numbers in **bold** refer to pictures and captions.